C000045525

OTHER BOOKS ON BEN HARTLEY

BEN HARTLEY

by Bernard Samuels

The first survey of the life and work of Ben Hartley,
illustrated with 60 paintings in colour with related
drawings from Ben Hartley's notebooks

Published by Sansom & Company

ISBN 1 900178 73 7

PIGS MUST EAT ON SUNDAYS

A delightful introduction to the notebooks of Ben Hartley

Edited by Bernard Samuels

Published by Green Books Ltd

ISBN 1 903998 68 9

The website www.ben-hartley.co.uk presents a
wide range of paintings and drawings as well as
Philip Cashian's *Six Pieces for Piano after Paintings
by Ben Hartley* performed by Thalia Myers.

£4.80

DEAR SUSAN
LETTERS TO A NIECE

BEN HARTLEY

Susan pictured in 1963

DEAR SUSAN
LETTERS TO A NIECE

BEN HARTLEY

Edited with an Introduction by Bernard Samuels

Sansom &
Company

First Published in 2011
by Sansom & Company
Pembroke Road, Clifton, Bristol BS8 3EA
email: info@sansomandcompany.co.uk
web: www.sansomandcompany.co.uk

Text and images © Bernard Samuels

www.ben-hartley.co.uk

Designed by Steve Hill

Printed by Latimer Trend and Company, Plymouth, UK

All rights reserved. No part of this publication may be reproduced,
stored in a retrieval system or transmitted in any form or by any
means - electronic, mechanical, photocopying, recording or otherwise
- without the prior consent of the publishers.

British Library Cataloguing in Publication Data
A catalogue record for this book is available from
the British Library

ISBN 978-1-906593-85-8

For Susan

ACKNOWLEDGEMENTS

I must take the opportunity to thank my friends Graham Morris, Adrian Ballisat and Neil Cooper for their unstinting help in bringing this project to fruition. I would also like to thank Keith Micklewright most sincerely for making his letters from Ben available to me when I began work on this book. Sadly, his wife Jane, a good friend and great admirer of Ben's work, died before I heard about Ben's correspondence with his niece. Above all, very special thanks must go to Susan Daniels for her insight and appreciation of her uncle which have provided the initial inspiration for this book.

The artist Ben Hartley was born in 1933. He grew up next to his grandparents' farm in Mellor on the edge of the Peak District. He is known for his gift as a colourist and the exceptional quality of his drawing. His work is widely appreciated for its humour and for the poetry conveyed by Ben's deep affection for country living. He is also known for his unusual practice of always painting in gouache on brown parcel paper.

A product of Manchester Regional Art School and the Royal College of Art in the 1950s, he moved to Devon in 1960 and taught part-time for almost twenty years at Plymouth College of Art. He lived in Ermington, a village eleven miles east of Plymouth. Though his means were extremely limited, he failed to make moves to sell his work. A significant change came about when he was introduced in 1976 to Bernard Samuels, Director of Plymouth Arts Centre who began showing his work and finding exhibitions for him.

In 1983, after his work in Plymouth had come to an end, he moved to Presteigne in the Border Marches, a town he had known since 1958. He lived there for the rest of his life in a house in the middle of the town within easy walking distance of a Carmelite Monastery. He had converted to Rome in 1968.

Throughout his life he suffered with severe bronchial problems from which he died in March 1996. In his will he left all his work to Bernard Samuels, a vast collection of over 900 paintings and 300 notebooks.

Ben Hartley being of such a private nature, it was very difficult during his lifetime to promote his work as strongly as it deserved. His extraordinary bequest has created an opportunity to remedy this shortfall.

INTRODUCTION

Ermington

28 June 1965

…I have applied to both the Exeter and Falmouth Schools of Art without being offered an opportunity either east or west (I am now quite out of date; I have certainly always been a little out of step.) And writing a children's picture story? – I have written many. Two books this year; and if my illustrated letters to my nephews and nieces were bound together also, - I would be the "worst seller" of the year, I'm sure.

Yes, the writing has all been for the family and has never been more than something to have alongside that morning's breakfast-time boiled egg and marmalade.

This characteristic extract comes from a letter Ben Hartley wrote to Keith and Jane Micklewright: Keith recently a colleague at Plymouth College of Art, Jane a fellow student and friend at the Royal College of Art. Ben was experiencing one of his occasional periods of uncertainty about the security of his teaching hours at Plymouth College of Art. Of course little would he know that one day his letters to his niece Susan would join the great mass of material he left me in his will, still less that some of these letters would be "bound together" into this volume.

Ben arrived in Plymouth in 1960. After leaving the Royal College of Art in 1957, though he had gained a first class degree and a high reputation among his contemporaries as well as those who taught him, his natural instinct was to get away from London, which he had detested, and return to his home territory in the Peak District. He lived at his parents' home in Mellor for the next three years and found some part-time teaching at his old art school in Manchester. Mary, the younger of his two sisters, both of them married, was living in nearby Hazel Grove, on the edge of Stockport, not far from the parental home. She had two children, a boy and a girl Susan, born in 1954. Ben, it would appear, saw a good deal of them and clearly took a keen interest. When he moved to Devon, devoted uncle that he was, he more or less immediately began writing to his nieces and nephews.

I first heard from Susan, now Susan Daniels, still resident in Hazel Grove, in March 2009. She wrote saying she would like all the letters – one hundred exactly – that she had received from her Uncle Bert to become part of the archive that has grown around her uncle's bequest. (Ben's first name was Herbert; in his younger days he was known to the family as Bert.) By July 2009 her plan was in place. With the letters came a whole collection of handmade birthday cards, Christmas cards, all kind of ingenious and amusing things made from paper – and two splendid story books.

The Ben Hartley I knew was an extremely shy and retiring person who spoke very little. Leaving aside the obvious charm of the writing and the illustrations, I was struck most forcibly by the ease with which Ben assumed the role of uncle. Susan's childhood memory is of an uncle who was always keen to set off for walks and take part in everything the family did. However, she does remember how very quiet he became later on in the 1970s, taking little part in family conversation: very much the Ben I got to know in 1976.

The thirty six letters I have chosen for this book are here simply because they are among my favourites. One could have included them all; any number would have conveyed their flavour. What emerges is a Ben Hartley with a true gift as an entertainer, a far cry from the quiet person I have described.

Each time he sat down to write to his niece he would find some anecdote or event in his life to turn into a little story to which he would add illustrations. Kindly, conscientious uncle that he was, he would always look for ways to make the letters educational as well as amusing, exploring history or teaching her about the natural world and country life which was so important to him.

When the correspondence began Ben was living in digs in Plymouth, looking for somewhere to live out in the country. Thereafter, apart from the two exceptionally beautiful letters written from a rectory in Norfolk, all the letters in this book were written from Ermington. One of the great delights of the correspondence is the picture of village life Ben conjured up for his young reader. For all I have emphasized Ben's solitary nature and his underlying sadness, he was by no means aloof. He was always extremely courteous and, as is evident from the letters, he was on friendly terms with his neighbours. In one letter he goes from lunch with one neighbour straight on to tea with another.

Two people, Dick Lang and Adrian Hall, feature quite prominently in the correspondence. Dick was clearly a 'character', well known in the village, who held a particular fascination for Ben. He was a rough, amiable fellow, sexton and chimney sweep, as Ben recounts: very much a local man but living some way off from the village itself. Adrian Hall, a Cornishman by origin, was a student at Plymouth College of Art where Ben taught, who lived in a quaint caravan parked in the grounds of Strode House, a grand house on the outskirts of Ermington. Adrian and his lifestyle are described for Susan in great detail. He went on to study at the Royal College of Art, became a sculptor, active in the field of the avant-garde. Adrian and his lifestyle are described and illustrated for Susan in great detail.

In spite of their marked differences, they both illustrate an interesting aspect of Ben's own nature, and very likely his own perception of himself: there is something of the outsider in both of them.

The quality of the writing in these letters, in fact in all his correspondence with family and friends, was of a high order. Every letter I have chosen here is in some way memorable; the expression *tour de force* often comes to mind. To list but a few: the early description of the chaos of moving house; the story of the fox that got away; the evocative description of life at a rectory in Norfolk; the hilarious account of a village hall slide talk about Africa or the beautifully imagined story of a carrier pigeon that found its way to the top of the church spire – all accompanied by their illustrations.

The last letter in this book was written at the end of October 1970 with Susan coming up to her sixteenth birthday. It has a distinctly elegiac note; "November written across my landscape" he writes, in the very first paragraph. And then he asks "You won't be too old to have a Birthday? You won't be too adult to write letters?" At which point he immediately switches to talking about letter writing in general, throws in a reference to Walter Scott ("Sir Walter Scott") and Abbotsford and then wanders off somewhat disjointedly, finishing up with thoughts on the supreme importance of life lived in the present moment.

Ben Hartley's letters to his niece are a sheer delight. They are also invaluable for what they tell us about an exceptional artist. The longer I have lived with his bequest the more I have become aware of the essential humanity of this very private person. These letters have greatly enriched my awareness.

For which I must thank Susan.

Bernard Samuels

Editor's note
The earliest letters written to Susan did not have dates. The dates shown were added by Susan some years later.

THE LETTERS

Dear Susan,

Thank you for the letter and the drawings - do keep well. It will soon be Spring and the sun will shine for you and all the flowers will be out. Then you will go to pick bluebells!

Last week I went to the sea - by the harbour - and all the boats. I saw two French fishing-boats.

Here they are. Do you
see the little dog?

The fisher-men had baggy trousers with many patches, and

stuck their hands in their pockets!
In the harbour were some big white birds swimming about.

They were swans.
There was also a
small boy in a boat all
by himself.

5/ Here is the fishing boat going to sea —
wave it good bye!

6/ This morning I had a big surprise — when I opened the door what do you think I saw in the garden next-door? I saw a life-size soldier with a sword and shield made all in wood. He looked very fierce! (He is an old ship's figure-head.) He did give me a shock.

To see what he looks like turn to page seven......

7/

"The Warrior"

Do you like his beard?

Give my love to
Michael. Is he always
a good boy?
With much love
from
Uncle Bert

X   X   X

1

Plympton
S. Devon
1960

Dear Susan,
Very many thanks
for your letter, the drawing
and the lovely mat. It is
very pretty - I like it very
much and have put it on
the sideboard for every-
one to see. You are a
clever girl to have
made it so well and so
neatly.
Yesterday I had a
ride on a tiny train - one
small engine pulling one

small coach. It was a chuff, chuff, puffing little engine - not a fast diesel. It went over high bridges and near a big moor - Dartmoor.

There were many Girl Guides on the train coming home and I saw a tent where some

boys were camping.
They had put the flag
up!

I think they were
boy scouts and were
having sausages for
their tea!

5/ On Thursday I was
by the sea and many
people had their swim-
suits on and were
bathing — but not Uncle
Bert — he was in his
overcoat!

6/ It was a lovely day
Spring was in the air
and all the birds were
happy and singing.

Singing about the
Spring tra-la!
With lots of love
from
Uncle Bert.

Plympton
S. Devon
1960

Dear Susan,
I think it is my
turn to write!
Thank you for
the letter. I am glad you
can skip so well and have
been to see Auntie Marion
and Catherine.
Whose cottage
do you think I saw the
other day? It was Old
Mother Hubbard's. Did
you know she lived in
Devon? Well, she did
and not far from here
at Yealmpton.

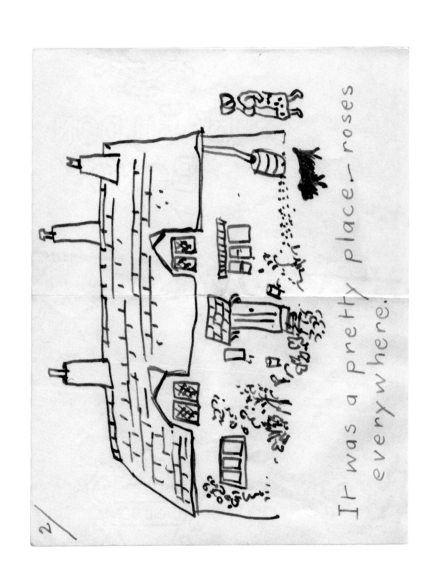

It was a pretty place—roses everywhere.

2/

on sunday I met a
thin cat with a long nose.
It was sat in a farm-yard
at Sparkwell.

It was watching the
birds fly by.   It was

thin. I think it wanted a drink of milk. It could not even "purr!" It sat and looked at me and at the birds in the sky then slipped through the gate and did not even say good bye.

What a funny cat! Would Michael like it?

On Wednesday I was
by the sea on Plymouth Hoe.
There is a lighthouse on
the Hoe

and a Grand Hotel. Also an
old castle — The Citadel.

The Citadel has a fine
gate way - built in 1670

From the Hoe I could see
ships and sailing boats
and one man was looking
at them through a tele-
scope.

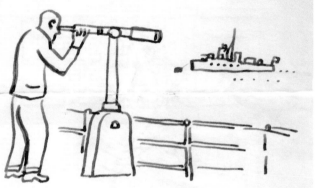

In the water is a
diving board for the
swimmers to jump from
into the sea — SPLASH!

9/ Like this –

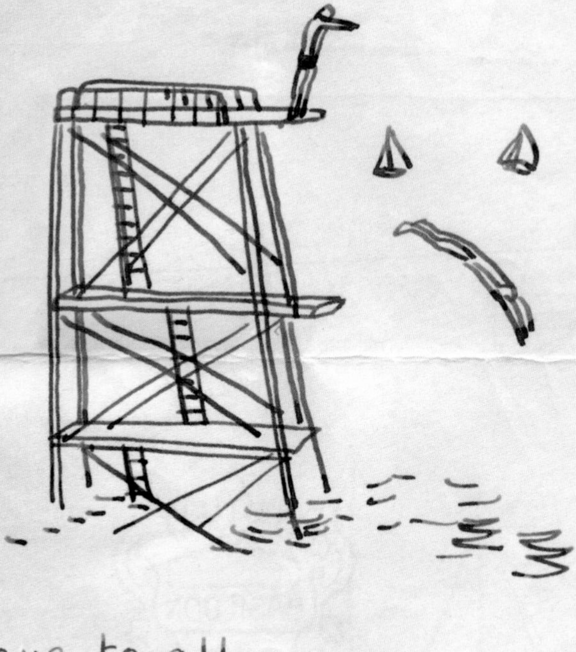

Love to all
at Norbury Grove
From Uncle Bert
x x x

Plymouth
Devon
1960
Dear Susan,
Thank you for the
letters and all the drawings
you have sent. What a
wonderful post it was for
my birthday!
You are good at letter-
writing. Your teacher will
be pleased. And I am very
pleased by all your drawings.
I love to see them. Do save
some to show me at
Christmas, won't you?
I have had four
birthday cards and they
are all on my mantel-shelf

over the fire-place.

Have I told you about the gas-geyser in the bath-room here? I have such a bother with it when I want a bath.

First the water is too cold, then the gas goes out— POP! Then I have to light the gas again and the water flows too slowly and U.B.H. is left

in the cold waiting with
only his vest on! At last
the bath is full. I test
the water with my toe
and it is too hot! Oh! Ow!
U.B.H. has then to wait for
the water to cool before.
he feels it is just right.
Then in I go! Splash!

with lots of love
to You and Michael

xxx
xxx
U. BERT

2 Boringdon Villas,
Plympton,
1961

Dear Susan,

Thank you for your letter and the drawings. I like them all.

I am glad you have been to Mellor and had a walk in Slackwood. Was there much water in the brook? Not as much as in the sea! Of course not!

I went to a place called Padstow, which is by the sea and saw a fishing boat and lots of little boats and people sunbathing on the sand.

I have also been to Salcombe where people go to fish and swim and sail and to sit in the sun.

When I went to see
Monica and Andrew I had
a long ride on the train
and saw lots of things
from the window —

A sand castle at Dawlish
and some one waving
to the train as it went
by.

This is a caravan
in Wales. People stay
in caravans for holidays.
They hook the caravan
to the back of the car
and off they go-pip,pip!
Anywhere they like
up hill or down dale.

Then the train passed
some tall trees with nests
in them. They were rooks'
nests, I think. The birds
said "Caw, caw, caw!"

6/

When the train blew
its whistle, it frightened
some ponies and off
they ran across the
field, as fast as they
could go. Gallop-gallop-
gallop with their tails
flying in the wind.

Then I saw some big
black-and-white pigs
that lived in a red shed.
They were feeding and
said "snuffle, snuffle,
grunt — grunt, grunt, snuffle."

"Snuffle, snuffle, grunt"

8/

In one field was an
old waggon painted blue
and red and along
came an orange tractor
which said "puff, puff
chug; puff, puff, chug."

This week I called at
the bank for some —

so that I could do my —

What a lot I had to
buy! Now my —
is nearly empty!

what did I buy?

11/ It was such a heavy load to carry. I could have done with Susan and Michael to help me! That would have been a help for Uncle Bert, wouldn't it?

Now all the shopping is put away in the cup-board and I need not do any more till next week.

With much love
from
Uncle Bert.
X X X

P.T.O.
My washstand! And hot water-bottle!

2 Boringdon Villas
Plympton
1961

Dear Susan,
        Should I tell you
where I went yesterday?
I had a long walk in the
sunshine to a church that
had a crooked spire. Yes,
it was quite bent! Not at
            all straight
            as a spire
            should be.

Spires should go straight up in the air, like this one.

2/

In the church were
two very old helmets
– hats that soldiers
used to wear years
ago.

Are not they strange?

It was a lovely walk.
The sky was blue, the
birds were singing
and I saw a butterfly.
Flowers were everywhere

4/ Near this church
I met some little boys
who had a dog called
"Nipper."

They had an old
swing to play on :—

5/ Then I had a ride on a bus, saw another old church and then came home. The clock on this other church was five minutes fast, so I had to wait longer for my bus. What a pity!

6/ Do you like the weather-cock on the tower? It tells us which way the wind is blowing. Let us hope it is a warm wind that will bring us the Spring.

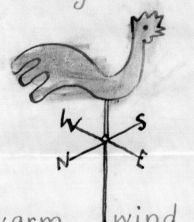

A warm wind from Devon bringing love from
Uncle Bert.

4 Wood View,
Ermington,
S. Devon

Dear Susan,
I hope you are
feeling well again — and bright
and breezy — not sneezy or
wheezy! Keep your chin
up — it will soon be Christmas!
Hurrah!
Have you seen my new
address above? I am now in
my new house and busy
putting everything in order,
before Christmas: things
have been a bit upside down.
like
this —

I have bought a bed, three chairs, a table and a kettle and a pan. The kettle looks well on my stove.

The scullery is ʊɯopǝpᴉsdn yet, I am afraid. It is full of everything - coal and carrots, cress and cups.

What a jumble! Where is my
shaving brush? Can you see
it in the picture? I shall miss
my bus! The alarm has
gone brrrrr!!!!!!
I must wash and  shave
and stoke the fire, make
the bed and comb my hair
and the is on its way from
Totnes! ^bus If I miss the
bus I shall be late for school
and the students will put
me in the corner!! What a
rush! Here is the green bus
98 for Plymouth at 7.45am

Off to Plymouth past Mother Hubbard's cottage: bright and early!

From my kitchen window can see two black pigs and white hens, also my two clothes lines —

The coal shed is on the left
– the dustbin on the right!
There is not a garden like
Daddy's – only one small
bed in the yard – just big
enough for some candituft!
And if I don't watch – the
weeds will grow – it is big
enough them!
        Keep smiling. You will
soon have the   up.
 With love
to you, Michael,
Mummy and
  Daddy
  from
  Uncle Bert
    x x x

4 Wood View
Ermington
1962

Dear Susan,

What is the name
of your milkman? My milkman
is Mr Lapthorne and he
lives at the hamlet of Penquit
two miles away. He is
always happy and cheerful
and tells you what a
lovely morning it is.

He has a farm and
keeps a horse to ride. It
is a retired race horse with
an unusual name and is
quite famous for it has
won many prizes and
lots of gold cups.

When the weather is cold or wet it always wears a coat to keep it warm and dry. Is'nt lucky?

Mr Lapthorne keeps pigs and four guinea fowl.

There were far more at one time, but the foxes took them. If any stranger comes near they make a great deal of noise and utter thrill cries of alarm:- a real hullaboo!

He also has some of those strange creatures - Muscovy ducks - how odd they always look, waddling about in search of insects, flies and little grubs.

Here they are
Quaack!

Would you believe it! It rained so heavily on Friday night that there was a <u>worm</u> washed under my backdoor! A wriggling red worm! So I put it in the garden to burrow down amongst my parsley seeds. I did not want a worm in the scullery!

There was another adventure on Wednesday. A cow tried to eat the clothes line! It put its head over the wall and chewed my clothes line!

So out I rushed to shoo it away! It must have been tired of eating grass.

Have you ever seen a cat with odd eyes? There is a huge white cat in the blue village that has one greeny^ and one pink eye – how odd!

Michael would love it! It

rolls on it's back for me to tickle it's tummy.

   The chimney sweep called on Wednesday and took all the soot from the kitchen chimney — giving it a real spring-clean!

   What colour are the eyes of a white rabbit? Can you guess?

with love to you all
from
Uncle Bert

4 Wood View
Ermington
May 17th, 62

Dear Susan,
        I am a naughty boy!
Two letters from Susan,
and none from Uncle Bert.
This won't do, will it?
        Thank you for them
both. They are well illustrated
and give me much pleasure.
I like the cat and the one
of the house and have them
both displayed on my table
near one of your mats.
Do keep up with your drawing and please some to
show me.   save

Do you know what a proverb is? How many can you remember, I wonder?

A ——— may look at a King.

It's no use crying over spilt ———.

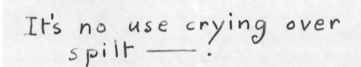

A ——— in time saves nine

A bird in the — is worth two in the bush.

New — sweep clean.

Don't have all your eggs in one —.

The early — catches the worm

4/

Don't count your —— before
they are hatched.

It's an ill —— that blows
nobody any good

The proof of the
—— is in the eating

No —— without
a fire.

You asked if I had a
table in my bedroom on which
I put books. No I keep mine
on the ledge beneath the
window in the kitchen —
library books on the left
and my own on the right.
it is an untidy collection
very often.

I have something new
in the little yard at the
rear. It's a tiny tub and

I have made some holes in the bottom and filled it with soil. Now there is a pansy growing in it. I am very fond of this old-fashioned kind of flower — I think it used to be called "Heartsease." I have also sown some parsley and spinach seed, and they are just beginning to come up — very, tiny little bits of green.

How does your garden grow? With much love from your old-fashioned bachelor Uncle Bert.

4 Wood View
Ermington
Oct 65

Dear Susan,
          Thank you for the
letter and all the drawings,
and telling me about school.
Do you learn any geography?
should we have a lesson?
          I enclose a picture
of Devonshire - the county is
famous for cider, cream
(clotted) and Sir Francis Drake
(he appears in the History
lesson) The view is from
the front bedroom window
of 4 Wood View and shows the
School A, the police-station B,
the bridge of the R. Erme C,

"Fawns", Mr Cox's farm D, and Ludbrook Manor E. This was built in the Middle Ages, a long time ago. Near the sky-line I have marked Higher Ludbrook F, the farm that belongs to the Churchwarden Mr Pinsent. G shows you where the trees hide from sight a fine old house—Strode Manor. There is a vast rookery there and what a noise the black birds make in the Spring-time. Caw-Caw Caw-Caw!

So there you see a Devon landscape—not so flat as Cheshire, lots of trees.

and plenty of rich, green
grass for the red Devon
cows to turn into milk,
and orchards growing
apples, baskets full of apples
to be made into Cider.

   The people have rich,
deep voices and always
call you "my dear." Only
they say "mi dear." How
are you "mi dear?" Like
that.

   I hope you are very,
very well, _my_ dear. And
will keep so all winter
through, till the cuckoo
comes back to Devon next
spring. Much love from U.B.H
      X X X

4 Wood View
Ermington
1962

Dear Susan,

　　　A Very Happy Birth-
day to You! Good Old
November the Fifth!
Have a Jolly Day and I
hope you blow all your
candles with the first
puff! Right out!

　　　What is the news
from Ermington? Let me
see. A student has come
to live not very far
away from here in a
caravan, the kind that used
to move around the country
with fairs and circuses.

It does make an unusual home – a little house on four wooden wheels stand under some huge trees where the rooks live. In other woǫǫrds – in a rookery – the rookery at Strode on the left hand side of the picture in the geography lesson.

He invited me for supper
and I found everything
very snug and cosy in his
new home, in spite of the
wind making such a noise
in the huge trees overhead
and an occasional tap-tap
on the roof. Listen – tapity-
tap! What do you think it
is? Only the acorns falling!

On one side is the
stove, all bright and shiny
with a mantel-shelf and a
mirror. There are books and

brushes and a beer mug full
of pipes - one for each day
of the week! And more

besides. Twenty two in all!

He also has a collection of hats — but never, never wears one outside! He says they are useful when cooking to stop his hair from getting in the eyes! Do you think he has a night-cap?

Hats, pipes
and boots
big BOOTS.
He has many
pairs and the
longest, and strongest he
wears when on his motor-
cycle, cycling to the
College each day.
There is only
just enough
space to get
them all in his
caravan at
home in the
rookery.

One Sunday I met a great
many grasshoppers. They
were jumping up and down
in the grass - doing a kind
of dance for themselves
in the sunshine

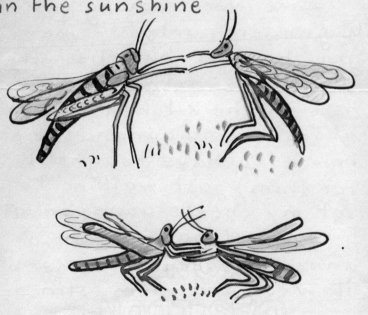

Some were having quite
a garden party. I like
grasshoppers —but flies —<u>they</u>
are a pest.   There is one
here in the kitchen—"Fred"—
who sits on a banana (he
thinks I have bought it
for him) just waiting to
eat my cheese as soon as
I bring it out. He is so
annoyed because I keep
it wrapped in muslin.
    He is lonely today

because last night, his big
brother Frank, (a proper
buzzing blue bottle if ever
there was one) fell into
Uncle Bert's cup of hot milk

— and he couldn't swim.
So poor Frank sank!
   Have a good time on
Monday, and like the fire-
works — may everything "go
with a bang!"
       Love and ×××
          from Ermington
             U B H.

4 Wood View
Ermington
1962
Dear Susan,
    Thank you for the
very pretty birthday card
and your letter and all
those kisses xxx you sent.
    No, I am not a
proffessor! I have not risen
to that rank!
    What is Pauls surname
you asked? It is Hill, Paul Hill.
What Mellor Church stands
on! Do you remember the
name of anyone else in the
village? Any of my neigh-
bours? Mrs House, who
lives next door :—

and the chimney sweep"
who is the
sexton as
well :-

here he is again:-
"Old Dicky" as he calls
himself! Mr Lang on
Sundays!

There is
only one
thing the
matter
with him
he says -

"he can't
get enough
Guiness!"

Some one going to Friday
night choir practice:

and not in a hurry!

Mr 'whats-his-name' crossing
the square with a basket
of vegetables :-

and a bag of
fertiliser :-

and the milkman on his
horse :-

Tally Ho!

And not
forgetting
your
loving
U.B.H.
x x x

4 Wood View
Ermington
Jan 1983
My Dear Susan,
       What a sweet letter
you sent me! And written in
ink, too! I was pleased to
have it. It really did give
me a BIG thrill. Thank
you.

       Yes, I did get back
safely, but it took me along
time. As there were no
buses running, because of
the snow, I had to walk
the last part of the way:-
in my big gum boots.

Fact

I found Devon deep in snow, and it is still here. In another four inches fell on Saturday night. The wind is from the east and blows right through you. It finds its way under the doors, into the house and creeps up my underpants!

Everywhere the view is white. Roads have been dug out with the help of tractors, like Mr Kenworthy's and the snow is nearly as high as a house on either side. Icicles hang over-head as long as swords & as sharp. The snowplough

came through the village
and swished its way into
the square yesterday
morning. It is all as pretty
as a christmas card—and
much, much colder!
     The poor birds—don't
you pity them? Nothing to eat
but what we put out for them.

The poor things are starved
to death and too weak to

fly from sleek-coated, well-fed pussy. It is a tragedy.
So all the Village is trying to feed them with whatever it can. The baker made a mistake and put too much caramel in his cake. So the birds have had 12 lbs of Christmas Cake to keep out the cold!

One rich old lady buys them

several Madeira cakes each
week as well as pounds and
pounds of currants.

I came back from my
Sunday stroll with my
pockets bulging with - guess-
¡S⅂IⱯNS! The thrushes love
them and I have cracked
each shell open with the
hammer and hav'n't the birds
had a treat! The wagtails

have had crumbs, the robins
 suet, sultanas for
the black birds, whilst
for the acrobats — the

blue tits, that is, there has
been a fine piece of ham fat.
The starling is a cheeky
fellow, and one nearly choked
himself, he was in such a
hurry to have the largest bite

The strangest sight
was to see a great white
owl, a barn owl, hunting not
in the night time, but in
the day light, it was so
hungry.   There it was;—the
white creature silently
flying over the white fields.

1

Yet I have seen a sign of Spring. There were lambs in the snowy fields on Sunday all of them skipping about the snow. What a cold start to life! All they had to keep them warm were their woolly vests!

Not like you and I, all wrapped up; layer upon layer- pullovers upon pullovers. We all look much fatter than usual, don't we?

You should see us in Ermington!

"Uncle Tom Cobleigh
and all!" Mrs Harper
has socks over
her wellingtons
to grip the ice.
The Colonel has
a big yellow
sou'wester &
flying boots.

He uses ski sticks to help
him through the slippery
patches.

That was what I needed
when I was taking the dust-
bin to the road, where it is
left to be emptied. I slipped
with my load and went
down flat!

Bump!
Fortunately there were no
cuts or breaks. A roadman
helped me and kindly
shovelled all the contents up
again. I was lucky.

So here I am by the fire,

Michael's photo. is with yours on the mantel piece and my bed is in the kitchen, ~~wh~~ where I can sleep warmly all night in front of the stove. Everywhere
∧ is cosy and convenient.

Now I hope you are still all very fit; That your toes and noses are warm and there is not a chilblain in sight! Love to Mummy, Daddy and Michael, and to Susan, too

What a pity Christmas passed so quickly!

xxx Uncle Bert xxx

4 Wood View,
Ermington,
1963

Dear Susan,

Today I found a celandine in flower and on Sunday, the very first primroses and sweet little snowdrops. I felt I _must_ write and tell you. I want everyone to know that the Spring _is_ coming.

Now thank you for the exciting drawing and your well-written letter. Full marks for both.

Just a week ago I was watching the local hunt, whilst out for a walk. All the riders were slowly

mounting the hill opposite
and the red-coated hunts-
man was tootling away on
his horn as he disappear
from view. I thought "Oh
dear", I have missed all
the excitement, I am too
late" - when what do you
think crossed the road right
in front of me? The fox
himself! He <u>was</u> a big one.

He did not see me, and when
he had reached the other
side turned back and retraced

his tracks into Mr Cox's
farmyard and then over the
stream and down into the
River where he paddled
up and down, up and down
so that the hounds would
lose his scent. After a good
long drink he lay down and
had a rest on a log in the
water. And all the time quite
unaware U. Bert was watching
from the bridge!

It was a thrill! All the
while he lay resting, the horn
was sounding in the wood on
the hill and the pack was
hunting all over the slope.
Then finally he rose and

I watched him slip along
the River bank and across
the fields to his den:-home
in time for his tea!

Yes, the hounds did not
find him and soon came out
of the wood looking hot and
thirsty - all their tongues
were hanging out. The
huntsman collected them
on the roadside and called
them by name as he cracked

his long whip over their
ears. One was called Bertha.
then off they set homewards,
up the long steep hill to
Ivybridge and the kennels.

Sometimes the hounds meet in the Square here, and the are horses and riders all over the place. The landlord comes out of the "Crooked Spire Inn" and everyone drinks a stirrup cup. Some ladies ride side-saddle. Then a blast on the horn, a clatter of hooves and they are off! Tally Ho!

Gee up Fanny and Bonny! Yoicks! Tally Ho from Uncle Bert.

Dear Susan,

The bookmark is a beauty! It really is. Thank you very much for sending it me. It ought to be framed. Thank you also for your letter.

I do hope you enjoy your Holiday in the I.O.M. The picture post card Mummy sent shows some fine scenery — I should like to see it all.

Last weekend I went to London and stayed with a real professor (you once asked if I was one!) He is

a professor of Painting
and has many letters after
his name — quite a row of
them.

  A.R.A. C.B.E. R.B.A. Hon A.R.C.A.

    All of which, I must say,
he really does deserve.

He is a lovely chubby, rather fat man and quite bald — a bachelor in fact! He lives at Clapham Junction in a tall, old house with a house-keeper, two cats and a tortoise called Abraham. One cat is named "Blackminster" and the other is "Collar-and-Tie," because his markings are in smart black and white.

There is a long garden in which Abraham lives and it is full of roses. My bedroom was at the top of the house and because the Prof. lives near the railway and the

Junction is one of the busiest anywhere in the country, I could hear a steady rumble of trains all through the night. It went on and on a continuous roar of electric trains at 60 miles per hour! Not a bit like Ermington! (In fact, it is so silent at night here that I can hear the cows put their tongues round the clumps of grass, bite them off and swallow them)

However, I was so tired after walking round London that the British Railways

didnot keep me awake. I slept
till the sun came through
the blinds in the morning.
   The Professor's is a really
wonderful house - full of
pictures and books and other
treasures. There are pictures
everywhere - up the staircases
and in all the rooms on each
of the four floors. There is
even a painting hanging in
the lavatory! And books,
books, books; volumes and
volumes. You won't believe
it, but there must be at
least fifteen collected on
the window cill of the W.C.!

Then there is the antique
furniture, huge German beer
mugs, medieval cake slices
and a whole collection of
other interesting things
that have been collected by
him. The house is as good
as an art gallery and a
museum — and yet it is still
a charming and friendly
home. I could spend hours
in each room just looking at
its contents.

Alas, my visit was
soon at an end; on Monday
I was on the Torbay Express
and speeding back to Devon.

Faster, and faster and faster till the train came to Newton Abbott. Then change for Totnes and on the bus again from there to dear little Ermington.

So here I am once more. The church spire is still very crooked, the pansies have bloomed in my little tub and the milkman has left two little bottles behind my gate.

It is wonderful to be back once more – for in my view Devonshire is much, much more enjoyable than the Great City of London!

Lots of love,   Uncle Bert

4 Wood View
Ermington
Nov. 17th. 1963

Dear Susan,
        Never has anyone until this
year sent me **two** cards for my 13th
of November! So thank you for them
both and for your letter.
        The birthday cards deserve
congratulations. I must say how well
you painted the sea scape; the ship
looks real, the sea appears wet and
the treasure is worth diving for. Is
the boat sailing to the I.O.M.? I
feel sure it is.
        Your second card depicts a
ship, too. Perhaps that one is bound
for Devon and will shortly come
sailing up the River Erme. At the
moment the Manx Maid would almost
be able to reach Ermington — the
River is so full after the recent rains.

2

Of course I don't know about the mast and funnels being able to go beneath the bridges. That is a difficulty, isn't it? You would have to perhaps sail a smaller vessel. Ask Daddy. I am only a "land lubber" and the nearest I get to the water is when I wear my rubber gum boots

These I needed the other evening when coming home through the wet, slushy fields in the pitch dark night. If I am on the Kings bridge bus and not my usual bus to Ermington, I must walk the last mile through the fields by the River. When there is no moon I am really "in the dark." Squelch, squelch - splash! Don't the owls hoot and screech! Ar'n't I glad to reach the hard road, and see at last the winking lights of the village.

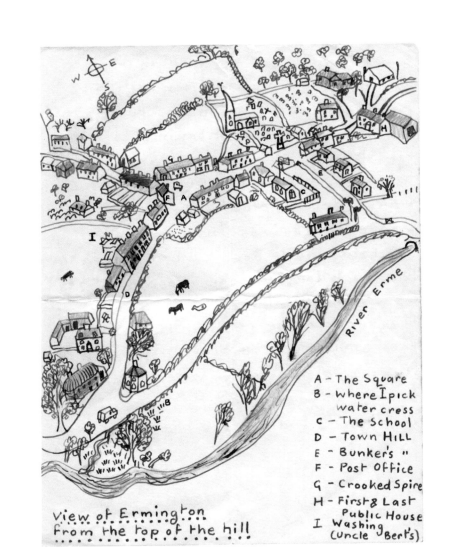

W E N S

H

A – The Square
B – where I pick
    water cress
C – The School
D – Town Hill
E – Bunker's "
F – Post Office
G – Crooked Spire
H – First & Last
    Public House
I – Washing
    (Uncle Bert's)

View of Ermington
from the top of the hill!

River Erme

4/   I hope you are well and warm,
Susan, and in your winter woollies!!!
I have shaken the moths from my
thicker vest this morning!!! and
feel fairly tickled back and front!
    The rain is coming down and
would drown elephants, believe me.
Larger creatures than worms will
no doubt have been swept beneath
the backdoor before morning. I must
be on guard. I cannot hear the
thunder for the rush of the wind,
the rattling of the stove pipe and
the gurgle, gurgle of water running
down the yard and into the drain.
"No picnics today" says the weather
cock.
    But Christmas is coming, says
Uncle Bert, and he sends you
loads of love and x x x x x.

4 Wood View
Ermington
1963

Dear Susan,
    I do hope you are
well. I have been thinking
about you. Are you getting
ready for Christmas?
I have been picking holly
and started to decorate
No 4. with red berries and
fire cones.

soon be breaking-up!

Yippee!

Do you know what the rain washed under my back door this morning and right into the middle of the scullery floor? A great long wriggling worm!

The scullery is full of things without anything else of the creeby - crawly kind! So U. B. H. popped it out in the yard in the parsley. I don't mind an odd black beetle and the spiders — but no worms, thank you,

On the other side is a view of the scullery about 7.00 a.m. showing U.B.H. getting ready for the day. Would you like to help with the washing-up?!! And on page 5 you see the other side of the scullery and the back door. It is a hitherto unpublished picture of the "Houses of Parliament!" Can you see where I keep the shaving brush and razor? The old zip bag on the left acts as a "linen basket." If you have a duster handy you might just remove that cobweb!

Let us open the backdoor
and see if the clothes are
dry. I left them out on
Friday night and by Saturday
morning the wild westwind
had tied them all up in
knots! So I had

better get out Grannie Towle's
irons. Love and xxx
Uncle Bert.

4 Wood View
Ermington
February 4th '64

Dear Susan,
        The pan-holder <u>was</u>
a surprise. Thank you very
much for making and sending
it me. My fingers were getting
quite burned — but now they
will be protected — it was
very thoughtful of you.
            I hope you are quite
fit and still enjoying all the
snow. What a white winter
it is! W for Winter! Brrrrr!!!
            Yesterday the sun
came out and so did your
U. B. H. I was invited to

have dinner with Adrian, the student in the caravan at Strode. There I sat in the sunshine with the top half of the door wide open to the view.

Very often, Adrian tells me a robin flies right inside to look for crumbs. Then it panics when it can't find its way out. Perhaps it perches on the pickle jar which you see on the table on page 3.

What a spread there was! Adrian cooked enough rice to feed half Hong Kong!

Afterwards I had to leave to go to Tea at a Farm

called Penquit. I did enjoy myself. Such a happy family live there - from Scotland.

First I had to go and see the lambs - all twins but one - out in the cold, cold snow. Then I watched Elizabeth sledging. She came down hill like an express train. The sledge had its name painted on the side -

FLASH

Her brother had made himself a pair of skis out of an old bed! What an affair! But it gave him some fun and not a few tumbles.

STUCK!

...

"Gillie" went with us and the
old sheepdog "Vick." Gillie is
a Dachshund — a German
"sausage dog" and loves to eat
dung! Poor thing walks with
a limp, as the car bumped

one of his short legs. No bones are broken and he will be able to run quickly very soon: — providing the snow is not too deep!

The farm house is very, very old - an ancient monument in fact. The fire place is the biggest I have seen — so big that you could burn half a tree trunk at once - without troubling to saw it up. It has a chimney to match. Two Father Christmases could come down at the same time! When I looked up I could see the sky at the top! What a blaze there was while we sat round foor tea. Gillie showed us how he goes to sleep lying flat on his back, legs in the air.

He was the only one to rest though. For afterwards all the family had to attend to their jobs. Mr Craig to go to the dairy whilst Elizabeth and her Mother brought in the ewes and lambs, John saw to the hens and David, the eldest boy milked the cows. All very busy except Gillie and your Uncle Bert. All I had to do was to walk back to Wood view in the moonlight <u>and</u> not fall into any deep, deep drifts.

Well, it has just stopped snowing and the world is white. It is just like living in Lapland! I think a team of reindeer will be needed to move the bus to Plymout in the morning! Or shall I hav to make a pair of skis!

With love and x x x x from someone who is'nt quite a Professor!!! (I wonder who that is!?!)

Penquit

4 Wood View.
Ermington.
1964

Dear Susan,
        Still smiling? Good!
And everything in the garden
Lovely! 🌸 🌸 🌸 🌸 🌸
        Last weekend — on the
Saturday — I walked to the sea
& back again. My path was by
the River all the way & the sun was
shining. What a perfect afternoon
I had.

        In the estuary of the Erme
(the mouth of river) I saw some
schoolboys paddling along in their
slim, little canoes; all in life-
jackets in case of capsize. But
what I really want to tell you
of was the boat I saw as I

came home. Michael would have
been <u>thrilled</u> to see it. I was
amazed. Never have I seen the
like. It was a raft.

Yes, a long, long raft, very
narrow & of great length & only
just (with the aid of two empty
petrol cans) afloat. It had once
been a footbridge, I was told; &
the crew sat (on the cans) one at
either end. The bows & the stern
looked the same to me, & the
Captain & the 1st Mate poled
their way downstream with
broom handles.

The Erme at this part was
just four feet deep, & the crew

— although clothed in shirts, pants & shoes etc, — did not hesitate to slip overboard if they thought the ship should be turned upstream or anchored. — Yes, the boys had an anchor, but I saw no lifebelts: so when they kindly offered to ferry me to the opposite bank (I had ended up in a boggy patch) I graciously declined. Do you think that was wise? I did. I prefer my bath in hot water from the:-
don't you? And besides that — I hadn't my towel.

Much love to all
at No 8   from V. Bent.

Dear Susan,

My pen is rested : it has now woken up, yawned once, stretched itself twice & is — I think — capable of sending three big X X X & all My Loving Wishes to you on your Birthday. Very Many Happy Returns of Your Day, Susan. May this Nov 5th be your Happiest Birthday yet.

Your letter was a real treat for me. Thank you. I hope you may never grow up so much that you no longer want to write to your old U.B.! Your writing keeps me young! But for it, I might possibly have a long beard, walk with two

and suffer from GOUT!

Your news is my tonic; & two tablespoonfuls from Susan — at regular times — works wonders.

A double dose, —— & I might be able to join the Brownies!

Now what can I find in the

Ermington Advertiser?

and Wood View Gossip

The Hunt met at the Crooked Spire

on Tuesday. On Wednesday the oddest
inhabitant scrubbed his livingroom
floor. (You should see me doing
this & in my old trousers, old shoes
& old hairstyle)

What a pity you haven't a
magic telescope; then you could
peep into South Devon whenever
you wanted a change of view.—
& you might see <u>me</u>! Yes, sat
at the table, pen in hand writing
to Norbury Grove,
Nr Stockport
cheshire.

Is that the correct address? I must be sure it is, for it would be a catastrophe if all my good wishes for The 5th failed to reach you. But I hope they will, & you will have the Bonniest Birthday ever.

And a double helping of
my Best Love,
Uncle Bert.

4 Wood View,
Ermington,
15th Nov. '64

Dear Susan,

What a lot of drawings & letters,
cards & love & xxxxx & Good Wishes!
I am quite overcome! Never have I
been showered with so many for
my birthday before. Thank you very
much — & especially for the book of
your paintings & pictures. I could
now have an Exhibition. Indeed
there is a great deal on show in this
room at the moment. It looks quite
festive. —— And all because I am
one year older.

How many white hairs are
there amongst the auburn? Not 31
I hope! Will you count at christmas?
So you enjoyed your Nov. 5th?

Please to remember
The Fifth of November,
Gunpowder, treason and,
— Susan Mary Towle
        ten years old & now a Brownie!

But I did not know you were a

Don't let anyone change you into

2 4   !

You are worth more than that.

        No, I didn't make a bonfire
or have any fireworks. But not so
my neighbours — Mr & Mrs Harold
House. Though they passed their

seventieth birthdays years ago, they also /celebrate The Fifth. So there were sparklers sparkling next door & cathorine wheels whirring! But at No 4 all was quiet —— & if there had been mice in the larder you would have heard them breathing, —— or nibbling!

Listen! What was that ? ? ?

4/   No, not the owl. Is it the
sound of the wind in the chimney or
that, of rain coming under the back
door? Perhaps there is a worm washed
onto the mat. I hope it remembers to
wipe its feet.

     Well, I would not choose to stay
out on a night such as this, so it is
welcome to a bed in the scullery. It
is time _I_ was putting my 🧢 on
and filling the H. W. B. too.

— I must be feeling my age!
     Good night then Susan
       & pleasant dreams
         & thank you for,
           all you sent
            to
        Your Uncle
         Bert.
          X

4 Wood View
Ermington
1965

Dear Susan,

Would it be my turn to
take the lid off the ink bottle and
open the writing pad? I do believe it
is, for in the letter rack I see a
letter from Susan which has not
yet been acknowledged. Thank you
for it – and for all the news of the
circus and its clowns and their capers.

How are you? Full of the
Spring, I hope and feeling like Hey
diddle-diddle and jumping the
Moon.

The primroses have come to
Ermington. The very first showed its
face on January 22nd and a week
later I discovered a celandine. The
lambstails are blowing in the hedges,
there are many snowdrops and for
the last seven days the skies have been

cloudless and, oh, so very blue.

On Tuesday I walked to Mod-
bury and called in the Barber's.
(You can guess the reason why.) In
steep Brownston Street I paused to
regain my 'puff' and looked at the
cobbler's window. The name is above :-

FORD

and behind the glass below are all
manner of objects besides the usual,
every day tins of polish, dog leads,
saddle soap and dubbin. There are
bridles and bits, a stuffed Red
Squirrel, the mask of a fox mounted
on a shield, and in the centre, next
to a Sparrow Hawk perched on a
small branch (alas, also stuffed) is
a replica of the leather-covered
rum flask carried by your Great

Grandfather on his foreign tours.
— It is just the same as the one he
took across Canada, down the Rhine
and to Palestine and the Pyramids.
I wonder how far this one had
travelled.

      Your new carpet will be most
handsome. I, too, have a new lamp-
shade — a pink and white one for my
front room. It should match the
hyacinths when they appear.

4/

Have you heard of the "Old Woman who lived in a shoe?" Well, I know a man who lives in a BOOT! You do, too. I have bought BIG, BROWN BOOTS. Each is as heavy as the elephant's foot and as waterproof as a walnus.

Their colour matches the Devon soil and is in harmony with your Uncle's hair.

Lots of love to my niece
from Uncle Bert.

Dear Susan,

I was much pleased
by your mid-March letter.
What a surprise — Joey's
feather.

Now if Master J. had
been a homing pigeon & not
a beautiful budgy (if that is
how you spell it) he might
have flown your letter to
Devon & saved you walking
to the post box. But I would
have had to very quickly
have written my thanks: he
would have wanted to

2/

return to you at once.
Possibly not even stopping
for bed & breakfast ——
perch or Rice Crispies.

Anyway if he should
decide to be a post_man_, tell
him to head for the gold
cock on the bent spire,
admire the view & turn left.
No 4 has a brown door &
the clothes line is always
there for him to rest his
blue wings. I will watch
the sky & only expect him
on a fine day & when the
wind blows in a helpful
direction.

Have you commenced

your Holiday? Have you ordered the Hot Cross Buns & double yolked eggs? It is almost six weeks since there were pancakes in the frying pan . . . . & perhaps you feel ready for a hot spiced bun.

Well, I hope you have as many as you can wish, & sunshine enough to allow them to be part of a picnic meal. Then a joyful Easter Sunday & a carefree, happy-as-can-be full-of-fun holiday to follow.

Here is love,
& lots of more love
from Uncle Bert.

4 Wood View,
Emington,
1965

Dear Susan,

Your letter gave me very much
pleasure;— you give me the news in
such a delightful way — always. I
feel transported to Norbury Grove
before my eyes have reached the
last line on page one. And by the
time I have turned over, I really
am right amongst those four-leaved
clovers & The Brownies.

2/ Well, what has Ermington to tell
you? Let me reach for my "thinking
Cap", & put it on —— there that is
better.

Yes, of course, last Thursday I
set out to walk along a railway
that wasn't there. It runs — or had
used to — alongside the R. Avon.
But when the B. Railways closed
the line two years ago, the metals
were removed, to leave a very

3/ pleasant track on which to walk
up or down the Valley. I walked down
the Valley several times, no last week
I thought I would walk up, instead.
And I did, until ——— I came to
where the railway crossed the river ———
or rather where it had used to cross
the river ——— for the bridge had GONE.
Didn't I blink my eyes! No bridge
I your Uncle B. can't swim!
I discovered that all the bridges

4/ (being made of iron) had been taken for
scrap. So up through the woods of
had to climb, & find another way of
continueing my walk. This I did & was
able to rejoin the old Great Western
further on.

It was a glorious day; the cuckoo
singing, the trout swimming in the Avon
& all the golden marsh marigolds
flowering on its banks. How I enjoyed
the walk.
   Of course when I came to a

5/ station there were only dandelions
waiting on the platform & earwigs in
the booking office; so I was nonplussed
to show my ticket. The waiting room
will still be waiting for the next train
.........next year.

"all change!" "all change!"
— to spiders' webs, birds' nests and
wild flowers.

Much love from the cider-shire,

Your odd Uncle Bent.
xxx old xxx

Dear Susan,

I was most pleased that your letter found the way to this new address, and was here to gladden my Monday Morning. Thank you very many times.

So Michael has carried the Train: & you are busy with homework. Have you all the correct answers? ✓ ✓ ✓ ✓ where is Norfolk?

Well, you don't need the atlas to tell you that this very large county lies in the east. Did you know that it was here that the Vikings

first settled? —— or rather
they sailed up the rivers &
looted & burned all the
villages & farms they came
to. How warlike they were.
Such pirates........ blood &
thunder & two-handled sword
    But, —— none of that
now: not in The Rectory. All
here is peaceful & quiet—ful &
serene & spacious. A Regency
Rectory in the country........
with gardens & glebe & orchard,
courtyard & stableyard, a
dairy, two staircases the most
beautiful views, & a Rector
who is the giant of a clergy—

man, with a huge sense of humour, ——————— & three little daughters plus one black dog.

Sally is the dog (eats anything from a hair brush to raw runner beans & oranges) and Susannah, Judith & Ruth are the young ladies. (Ruth being still in her high chair, or as she would say, — "me too little") — what a family we make. Then there is Mr Jeremy Oakes-Ash, too; & on the top floor with a room having a dormer window (what is that?) is your Uncle Bert's private, little nook or cranny.

Down in the kitchen (once

4/the butler's pantry) you will find Mrs Rectory & meet Elsie who brings our eggs (from our own "egg tree", — as the Reverend says!) Elsie rides up to the gate on her bicycle ~~on~~ three mornings each week & is very useful in every possible way you can think ~~g~~ of.

Can you picture my new address from that? Cornfields in the front of the house & a garden (with a HA HA [look that up!]) & a gleble field to the rear. A spinney lies to one side & the walled garden is situated on the other.
Ah — this is where Mr Colbey

5/ the gardener, must be introduced. He comes each Monday to make sure we don't need to buy vegetables; digs plants & weeds, & drinks his tea without any milk in it.

There are fig trees, pig-sties, stables & a study; two front gates & from the bathroom across the passage I have the most extensive view anyone ever had from his bath —— I feel sure!

All the windows (apart from those in the attic) have folding shutters, & in the servant's hall is a line of bells that

were not long ago connected
to each room in the house.
Ting-a-ling "Ah, Butler, will
you get my bath ready?
And I think the Canon (he
used to live here) would like
a sherry." Can you imagine
all this? Chandelier in the
hall (hanging from a heavenly
blue ceiling) & a table in the
kitchen which has only three
& three quarter legs.

7/ There are two churches to attend as the Reverend is in charge of both the parish of Northrepps & the parish of Sidestrand. From Sidestrand's round tower you can spy the sea: from the church of St Mary at Northrepps —— the fields of stubble & sugar beet, & the factory for —— turkeys!

I am half a mile from the village (one pub one shop), & only three miles & a bit from The Gem of the Norfolk Coast —— Cromer. Also only one inch from the foot of this page :— not much room for a drawing is there? We will have to P.T.O

I write sideways — longer lines but few of them. Phew! So ———

Here is the rectory seen from the road to Northrepps village in the county of Norfolk, and **all** the best love he has on Tuesday evening October 12th 1965 from your Uncle Bert.

The Rectory
Northrepps
Cromer
Oct 1965

Dear Susan,

The wind is in the trees:
& this afternoon I have been
listening to its whisper —
whispering of November.......
Soon it will say THE FIFTH,
I will blow — I hope — a
whole heap of Birthday
Greetings beneath the front
door at No Eight. May mine
join them in wishing you
the Very Happiest Birthday
to date: Good Health, Good
Luck & Full Marks all the
way ✓ ✓ ✓ ✓ ✓ ☆

I do hope that next Friday
gives you lots of thrills, &,
the biggest slice of cake.

Well I must now tickle
my top knot & scratch my
cranium with a sheet of
blotting paper; & try to tell
you more about life in the
Rectory attic — or my "nest"
(for my view is of the treetops

& next door to Mr <u>Oakes</u> - <u>Ash</u>)
I am high up & far off! The
attics are many, & one is full
of —— lumber: full of everything with which to start ten
Jumble Sales.

Yes, & in the little room
in which I keep my trunk &
my suitcase, you will find
many white & faded placards
that tell you about past
village fêtes: have a look!

PONY RIDES
6ᵈ A RIDE

←LADIES↔

ELECTRIC BELL 2ᵈ

WHERE DID HE DROP IT?
FIND IT, AND IT IS YOURS

.PAN
.LLEY
ALLS 3ᵈ

HOOP-LA
5 RINGS 6ᵈ

LUCKY DIP
3ᵈ a dip

TH CLUB
WHITE ELEPHANT STALL

HORSE BOXS
BY THE
OTHER GATE
PLEASE

ANKLE
COMPETITION
2.35 pm 6ᵈ

What reminders of sunny
Summer days ...... just think:—
"ankle competition" 6 d! & who
found the Hidden Treasure?
If you need a white Elephant,

5/ you will have to come & follow
this sign **TO THE FETE** →
Before you leave: what about

MAP
of Northrepps

where did he
drop the Chocolates?
3ᵈa try

What puzzles & prizes: & all
solved & won years ago.

Hark! what do I hear?
"See amid the Winter's Snow"
— Susannah is playing her
recorder & its notes have floated
up from the dining room &
through my deep mauve
painted door. What an unusual

colour that is. But it suits
the cowslip yellow walls &
my silver birch carpet, —— &
reminds me of stewed black-
berries with cream.

The walls of the hall are
painted a vivid RED, the front
door is GREEN & outside are
the columns of the porch which
are both WHITE. At first I
was quite dazzled: even now
I shiver slightly, when going
into the Community Room I
am surrounded by four walls
all BLUE. This Rectory is a
rainbow!

And where the rainbow
ends, —————— there is a crock of

7/ GOLD (or so t is said) up &
downstairs I may search —
amongst the six attics & their
oddments, & in & out all those
outbuildings (where in the
laundry you will find MOLE
TRAPS!) the coach house & the
dairy, the lamp room & all
those dark & chilly pantries — Ugh!
But; —————— what if this
rainbow _starts_ in Northrepps
& only _ends_ in —— Norbury
Grove at the magical number
EIGHT! Who knows?
    May you find the real
treasure on the FIFTH, Susan;
& may every blessing be yours.
    My best love
        from your odd Uncle B.

4 Wood View
Ermington
24. 1. 66

Dear Susan,

How are you? I have
been wondering....... How
is Hazel Grove, the School,
& The Brownies, — how are
they?

Can you tie a reef knot in
the dark with your hands
behind your back? Yes?

Or without matches & paper
light a fire in the middle
of a wet wood & make me
a cup of tea before I can

²/count ten & say Brown Owl?

Hurrah! To whit—tuwhoo!
        Well, when I was in
short trousers & the Boy Scouts,
— I was a member of the
CUCKOO Patrol. My shirt
was green, my hat was
broad & I always carried
little whistle.

Now; my trousers are longer

3/ & I am a Man Friday.

As I gaze out from my deserted island over the waters of the Erne, I see neither sail nor smoke in sight. This is my fifth year of solitude .... there are only Two tins of baked beans remaining.

4/ <u>But</u> the Treasure is found! It ~~is~~ was here all the time! Hidden & waiting & mine! Acradabra, Ureka but HALLELUJAH!

If you have a Union Jack : tie it to the chimney pot. I will wave my second best pyjama trousers in the trade winds & send you my warmest love in the next empty bottle I can find.

Here it comes
floating from far away
& your
Uncle Bent Monday

4 Wood View,
Ermington.
13·2·66

Dear Susan,
        Your pages were a
pleasure to me: thank you
for them all & for the flags
& the Brownie News.
        What news can I give
you? What to tell you—
yes, I know: After Evening
Class: My Walk to the Bus.
        This is really exciting:
Down a steep, narrow lane
past the Bethel Mission I
go; down, down again a flight
of stone steps beside the
Trinity House Pilot's Office which
brings me to the exact point
from where the Pilgrim Fathers

2/sailed to America (when? ask michael for this date.)

There a moving lights reflected in the harbour water & singing can be heard from the many taverns by the Fish Quay. Thumping & a-bumping come from the Admiral McBryde; Yo Ho Ho from The Navy, & the Jack Tars in the Crown & Anchor sound "Bound for the Rio Grande." The shadowy shapes move across windows, & behind dark, tall bottles I see

3/ unknown faces looking out.

I must watch my steps
— & the time. Careful now
over all these ropes by the
fishing fleet & mind the
wet fish, the slippy fish, the
smelly fish & the fishy boxes.
And don't catch your turnup
on the anchor of Gertrude
PH 410. Ouch, that was a
halibut's head — nearly

4/ brought our land lubber
head-first into the harbour.
Then I would miss the boat
——— I mean the bus.

   Ah, the clock on the
Custom House reads nine
o'clock. Across the Parade &
past the Indestructible Paint
Company I swim — sorry,
mean hurry, & climb the
hill to the bus station.
At the top there is a plaque
which tells me that Sir F.
Drake once owned a house
which stood on that spot:
I can read the date as I
pause for breath.

   Then round the corner

5/ I put my sea legs at the double: over the road, & in less time than it takes to say Armada I & my bag are all aboard the green bus for Ermington.

Nine nine, —— & the bell rings: the course is east by North East & we are off. Ermington ahoy,

Bon Voyage,

Up with the anchor, & Good Night, Sweet Dreams to you

from

Your lubberly landsman
Uncle Bert.

Dear Susan,

Your letter of Norbury News needs all my thanks. I did enjoy each line on every page & also your drawings.

Have you ever seen a cockroach as big as a COW? As long, as broad & as high? On Tuesday evening I saw such a creature ———— The COLXOSSAL COCKROACH! Direct from blackest Africa & in Ermington's Reading Room. Did I run away?

2/ well, no ——— I eat in
the dark, & watched this
magnified creature darken
the missionary's picture of
the middle of Africa. From
my chair at the back I
saw coloured slides of the
faraway natives between
views of our local ladies'

3/hats.

africa came to Ermington,
—— then on went the lights
& off went

4/Cuthbert Cockroach: he did not want a cup of tea. Oh, yes —— there were cups & cups of tea from a teapot as big as the map of Australia.

—— it held, I am sure, as much as the Indian Ocean. The sausage rolls _did_ squeal

5/ when they saw it spouting.
Most of the biscuits were
quite shattered, & some had
to be put back in the tins
at once. Of course, that is
the result of having Scream
Crackers .... Now if they
had been Rectory Rock Buns
—— the refreshments would
have behaved as calmly as
the Macclesfield canal.

But those sausage

6/
rolls going the wrong way
really, put the Maids of Honour
in the hot water. You should
have heard them cry out —
perhaps you did?

I dashed to the door,
the Africans had already
gone & even the cockroach
had quite disappeared. I
was the first OUT; — so what
finally happened is to me a
MYSTERY.

— deep in every sausage
roll.

So do watch them Susan
— they may need MUSTARD.
A big helping of
love from U. Bert.

Ermington
31 March '68

Dear Susan,

At last: I can sit down
& take out the &
thank you for your descriptive
letter. I didn't know you had
sniffing dogs or "impertinent
children" at Hazel Grove. I do
hope there are no further "ordeals"
on the way to school ———
not even half a thought about
mental mathematics. Forget
the fractions too: just count the
crocus.

The primroses here are
rather late this year. Though
the weather really is more

like May than the end of March. Quite lamb-like.

I have been up the hill this afternoon, past the Old Cider House up the narrow lane, & climbed by the Ruin to gaze at the view:

Hills & valleys, fields & woods, church tower & spire & the river curving round to the sea. Then

3/ down to a dear old farm where
the orchard is golden with the
wild daffodils & the rooks are
nesting in the tall trees. Back again
over the hilltop fields & home by
that very steep hill that passes
the Co-operative Farm Cottages &
brings you out at The Crooked
Spire in The Square.

    Can you picture U.B.'s
stride down the hill? Good: I don't
need to include a selfportrait.

    But the people I meet are
worth framing. You would love
our Ermingtonians: they are
worth a gallery all to themselves.

    Yesterday I talked with
Mr Lang (He was seen crossing
the right-hand side of the Square
on your Birthday) Look at his
bluebell eyes & the best beard

south of Bideford. He usually wears a few primroses in his hat & just now there is a spray of "Fuzzy" willow in his button hole. The pollen is going to gild the grey whiskers.

He has nearly four miles to walk before he is home. And the hill is long, & as steep as the side of a triangle that you meet in a theorem which I have forgotten & can't spell. Sorry.

My geometry has left me. Where was I? Oh yes. Coming down the hill, tramp, tramp, tramp; the larks singing, the lambs bleating & the sky advertising Dolly Blue. Turn right in The Square, & we will be back where we started from on Page 1 ———
Love from one at No 4

4 Wood View
Ermington
25 June '68

Dear Susan,

Is your hay all in? Or
perhaps you have not had to
use your umbrella this weekend.
I hope not.

I waved good-bye to Granny
Grandpa last Wednesday
morning, & by the time I had
travelled back to Ermington
from Totnes Station, shaken
the tablecloth & emptied the
teapot, —— down came a
drizzle. All change from the
sun lotion: why did I discard
the old sou'wester?

Rain on Saturday, rain

You Monday, & on Tuesday morning I feel like a lone yachtsman in the middle of the Atlantic. The Erme — I can see — is big & brown & pretending its the Amazon.

I hope the Mersey is in its rightful place & you are all very well, very happy & not bothered by end of term exams..

Dear me. The longest day has passed. Midsummer Day 1968 has left us.

Last night was grey, gusty & wet. Do you know what happened? — In rain, storm & wind & without

3/ even a parachute. U.B.
climbed into the Crooked Spire
——The Crooked Spire (original
& best) not the Crooked Spire in
the Square which opens at 10.30
& closes at 2.00 pm.

The only disappointment
was an absence of owls & bats,
& the visibility (which certainly
was poor on such a night).
But the adventure was not
to be missed.

The tower is a narrow one.
The staircase reaches only to
the floor on which the clock
rests, & above that there is an
ancient oak ladder to the
first set of bells (six in all).
Between this & the upper bells

4/ the way up is more awkward.
But I was not alone. The clock-
winder who was my guide
showed me what to do.

Before you could say
"Ding Dong" he had leapt
among the ropes & crawled
up the framework on which
the bells are slung & crossed
from one bell to another to
finally emerge at the very top.
And he did this as easily as
a cat might . . . .
The bells, of course, began
to rock as he climbed across
them . . . . . there was the
faintest, faintest chime
as he stepped from one to
another.

5/   Well, before I bore you by
my belfry, I must tell you that
the inside of the spire (I actually
reached it) is completely hollow.
It is whitewashed & rather like
the inside of an upside-down
ice cream cornet without the
ice . But all made of stone .
      And you don't realize that
you are far from the ground
until you crawl through a tiny
trap door & look out over the
low parapet & see the village
you have left behind . All
the houses, the school & the
square have shrunk . Look up!
The spire is very bent & the
weather cock, a whopper.
      Fortunately we ~~we half~~

6/
reached the lower floor of the
tower before nine o'clock. I was
glad to be below the bells
before they struck nine times,
& feel my feet on firm ground
& take my courage out of both
hands. The way down was not
so frightening as the journey up.
        What goes up : must come
down. —————— Unless you are
a bat or a barn owl. Even
weathercocks come down to be
regilded once in fifty five
years. What a draughty life.
North, South, East, West;
think of a number, add four
Wood View &,
        my answer   U.B.
            is Love from who?

4 Wet View,
You-know-where,
Today,
Nov 1968

Dear Susan,

Do you feel older? A day,
a year, a young lady? Of course!
May you have a happy Birthday,
& happy year & lots of Joy.

Lots of joy to you, & I am
sure you will give lots of joy, to
everyone else, — wherever you go.
For the Fifth of November: Hip, Hip,
H U R R A H !
Three cheers for Susan ! ! !
Sorry; Fourteen cheers for Susan !

I can't draw a cheer: what
does one cheer look like? well,
multiply it by 14 & there you
are —— full of cheer.

Now Uncle B. please; less nonsense. Not being able to draw a cheer at your age. Really! You ought to ashamed of your lack of _____ . cheer?

Have I thanked you for that neat, newsome letter you sent? It was very nice. You keep your writing to scale, ─ unlike my spread.

The full stop you see above is a full stop: it isn't a puddle (Did you think so?) The puddles are all outside at the back door, & grey in colour. The marigolds are nodding there their wet petals & the seagulls (I think) have gone to buy themselves umbrellas. Do you know what

3/ a half-set greengage jelly looks
like? If you do,—then you have
a picture of my old green felt hat.
It got wet this morning.

I hope you didn't.

Once upon a time — when I
was in Ireland — I really did get
wet.—And right in the middle of
a heatwave, too. Such a day it was.
Absolutely perfect........ I had
clambered up the side of a small
mountain, met some goats who
didn't want to talk to me & decided
to visit a tall castle in the distance.
This was tiring. The day was perfect.
I lay on my back in a field &
gazed happily through the ~~tall~~
grasses at the castle, & the sea &
mountains & the islands........
& the blue sky.

4/   When all at once, down came huge drops of rain on my face. Splash!

I was off; & raced for the Castle like someone pursued. Splash! A deluge! It was the only shelter; & I rushed to the fortress with a burst of interest in Irish Military Architecture.

5/   I studied Irish Military Architecture all afternoon (& ivy, & rushes,
& raindrops) all alone & out of
the way, as far as possible, of the
wet.   Ballycarbery Castle, Co. Kerry
Can I forget you?

    I can see that long, long
empty, shining - wet road back to
Cahirciveen .... feel the
rain down my neck .... & the
squelch of my shoes ⸺ squelch,
squelch, squelch ⸺ back to
Murphy's Bar. And no one else in
Kerry saw rain that day. It was
a local shower: Purely local. ⸺
Pouring down on the road from
Ballycarbery Castle to Murphy's Bar.

    Makes me feel glad to be by
the fire .... with my slippers on.

6/ Are you snug? dry? — has
anyone pulled your hair? Fancy
the Fifth of November coming round
again . . . . where would we be
without our birthdays? Where?
    Well, I hope this Fifth is a
very happy one for you Susan,
And November behaves ~~especially~~
especially kindly towards you.
No fog, No smog, No 'flu, no snew.
——————————— that last word
looks Norwegian. What can it
mean?
    I have no Norwegian dictionary
so will have to guess. S?N?
All I can think of is S*S*N
Guess right; & know I send
you lots of love,
    & every wish for a
        Happy Birthday
                    Uncle B.

4 Wood View
Ermington
Ivybridge
17. 11. 68

Dear Susan,

Your big, beautiful Birthday card arrived on the 13th,
also your letter. Thank you
very much.

You had quite an array
of birthday presents. I presume
you listen to your radio whilst
in the bubble-bath before
putting on the new pair of pyjamas.
You can sign the postal order with
the two pens & put some money
in the blue hold-all. Bob-your-
Uncle.

Do you know I have a
new hat? The size is LARGE
& the style waterproof: voilà

2/

Will it suit me? Will you wish
to borrow it ———————— & leave
the umbrella at home?
   I bought it in Plymouth last
week. The shop is old & dark, &
looks as though it catered for
Captain Cook. Or Grace Darling.
(Granny Hardley calls
a "Grace Darling.")

3/ " Got your tea-drinkers on ?"
Can you guess what that means?
Well, I have a rather heavy step:
tramp, tramp, tramp. Two of my
pairs of shoes have metal tips
to the heels. Naturally they
make quite a noise. You can hear
me coming.

My neighbour (four doors
away) is blind. He lost his sight
in an accident many years ago.
But he has a splendid vegetable
garden & brings the newspaper
each morning. Also preaches at
the Methodist church. He can
always recognize my step. One
day when I was wearing a pair
that is tipped at the heel with
rubber, he asked if I had my
"tea drinkers on."

In the old days when every-

4/one wore stout, heavy boots,
lighter shoes were only worn on
Sundays. Perhaps it was ale
on weekdays, tea on Sundays.

Mr Harper is the blind man's
name. He is as cheerful as a black
bird on a Spring morning. One dusky
late afternoon last month, I met
him going out of his gate, stick
in hand: "be just going black-
berrying", he said "see 'em better
in the dark." I did laugh.

He is making me a hearthrug
And he is very skilled at repairing
chair & stool seats with cane.—
you know the kind of work
under & over, over & under.

How is the health? I do
hope Good. No fog, smog, wheezes
or sneezes. Breath in: hold it.
               Love from Uncle B.

4 Wood View
Ermington
30.4.69

Dear Susan,

I was delighted to see your old hat.——it looks a knockout. Let me know if it suits you. But I am sure it will..... And should you ever want another I have a couple of beauties which could easily be posted,—— stuffed with primroses. Or do you prefer your hats to be decorated with violets?

Some weeks ago I put a lovely green one in the dust-bin. It had a big brim, & dyed ~~green~~ mauve would have been dazzling. Dear me! what a waste!

Your letter brought me
all the news. Thank you for
writing so fully. I am glad
you enjoyed your holiday.
   The weather was lovely,
wasn't it? I think E mington
had eight consecutive days
of sunshine. When I had
dusted & polished, mopped &
cleaned, I walked down thro'
the woods & sunned myself
on a fallen pine tree over-
looking the river.

3/   The views were poetical ———
how wonderful to sit down &
write a poem .... but I
cant.
" Oh to be in Ermington
   — now that April's there ."
Dear me! The date is May.
Time has moved on on the Church
clock since I sat down & con-
gratulated you on that new
hat. I am writing on Sunday
4ᵗʰ May, this year, to my niece.
   +   +   +
what can I tell her ? ? ? ?
Dear Susan, I have bought
——— you will be pleased to
know this ——— a new pair of
BRACES. They are green, & stretch
in both directions. You should
see them. They were very ex-
pensive: in fact they are the

4/ best braces. Even the March
Hare would admire them.

Perhaps the Mad Hatter
could make a riddle out of them.
"Why is a pair of braces like
the Month of May?" —— Think
that out please & write the
answer on the dotted line:——
. . . .
in green ink
The cuckoo came last Sun
day. He is in tune. The swallows
skim over the hedge-top black-
thorn & cherry blossom, &
gliding on the River this morning
were two proud white swans.
I walked through the green
fields & the birds sang, the
lambs baaed & from the farm
in the bottom of the valley came
the sounds of milking time.

5/ "Oh to be in Ermington......"
now that the Queen Mother is
coming along the Turnpike Road
this week, & is to stay at
Mothecombe House ——— just
where the River meets the sea.
I hope she will enjoy her visit
& like all the views.

I must ~~where~~ wear (sorry) my best cap
each day ...... I may have
to raise it .... & ~~bow~~
simultaneously. (Good thing I
have those new braces.)

My friend with the beard
(Mr Lang) now carries bluebells
in his lapel, & a bluebell in
his hat band. I wonder if the
Queen Mother will catch sight
of him? I am sure he is
patriotic.

If only the Primary School

6/ flag pole had not been taken down, ———— the Headmist might have shown a Union Jack.

Really it was the plumpest flag pole I have ever seen. It was too fat: it became rotten inside & had to come down I felt sad. Can you imagine the misery of being a fat flag-pole? Perhaps the children laughed at it?

Well, Susan, if this is not a load of nonsense (+ spelling mistakes) you had better write & tell me. I call it "old hat" —— from your old huncle Herbert lovingly X

Down by the River
under the trees
at Ermington
7. 9. 69

Dear Susan,

How very sweet of you to
write & wish me a welcome home.
Your letter slipped under the
door on Thursday morning —
my ~~day~~ first morning back. This
was really very thoughtful of
you: to say hallo on my first
day back in Ermington.

Yes, I had a safe journey.
The train was only about ten
or twelve minutes late at Totnes
(it had a rest in the middle of the
Severn Tunnel) & after an icecream
& two cups of tea at the tiny tea
room at the station I reached
No 4 at 6.20 pm.

All was safe, dry & the
garden tidies than I have ever

2/seen it before. The gardener
had been my neighbour: Mrs.
Kettlestring.

Ermington is still by
the River, the church spire is still
crooked & in the blue Autumn
sky the sun is shining. All
looks lovely.

Now I have enjoyed reading
your collection of Poems and
Rhymes, Susan. Quite my kind
of anthology. Edward Thomas
——I always like his writing,
& this piece of Irish gaiety by
Seamus O'Sullivan is most jolly.
John Arden's The Lobster Pot is
quite new to me. Did you know
W. H. Davies had only one leg
& was a tramp? (Do read his
Autobiography of a Super Tramp)

3/   Talking of Lobster pots takes
me back to a place in Clare
on the banks of the Shannon.
Through my window at Cappa
I had a lovely view of the
River —— Islands, Round Tower
& all.

        In the garden below my
bedroom window was a mountain
of —— what could they be? Wire
cages they appeared to be. Could
they have come from a battery
house for hens? But they had
coloured plastic objects (round
& with holes cut in them) in
the side. Then one evening!

spotted a man taking the
bottom out of a blue plastic
bucket with a knife. Also he
was cutting holes in its side.
He was making an entrance to
his home-made lobster pot!
How cunning: the puzzle solved!

Lobsters are probably partial to
pale blue. Or could the cages
have been for crabs? They were
not for kippers, anyway.
        What a beautiful day! The

5/ fish leap in the river + fall back with a heavy splash. I

see ripples, hear the plop, but always miss the fish. I saw five young ducks float under the bridge this morning. This afternoon there is a SHOW for Working Terriers + Family Dogs which is organised by the local hunt at Ivy bridge. Under the September sky I see that many of the stubbles are already brown + the ploughman has already been at work.

The days are shortening...
Therefore: Autumn Reading _____

6/   I am sending the sequel to
The Beautiful Years. Dandelion
Days has long been one of my
favourite books, & I do hope
that when Susan has quite
finished all her homework (all

of it) she may be able to sit
back & read about someone
else's schooldays.
    I bought this copy during
the summer holiday almost twenty
years ago, —— on Loch Awe
Station (see Scotland). The book
has meant much to me: Both
of us are fading. The description

of school life is so authentic.
Oh dear! Those crammed desks
& dried up ink wells, torn masters'
gowns & yellow wooden rulers:
the smell of gym shoes & an
apple core at the bottom of the
leather satchel . . . . . the honor
of being half a minute late.

Do young gypsies attend
school? On their curriculum :—
how to bake a hedgehog in clay?

I dare say they are quite without
clocks or watches, minutes or
half minutes. Only the sun could
make _them_ late, —— or early
& up with the lark.

Enjoy the Dandelion "hours"
& my love from V. B.

4 Wood View
Ermington
Ivybridge
31. 10. 70

Dear Susan,

The sky is dark, & rain is
sweeping across the Valley of the
Erme. November is written right
across my landscape. Only a
few days to go & then you will
be having your hair pulled.
Ouch! "Penny for the Guy" &
Susan's Birthday.

You won't be too grown-up
to have a Birthday? You won't
be too adult to write letters? No.
in fact the older one grows the
more letters there are to be written.
Love letters, letters to pen friends,
boy friends, school friends, girl-
friends, butchers, bakers, ___
candlestick makers — they all

I/ need "Dear Sir or Madam" & a sheet of paper & an envelope. This Waverley Paper sounds as though you might be addressing a letter to Sir Walter Scot at Abbotsford.

What books have you been reading? Or does homework mean you must put them aside till holiday time? Have you had a midterm? walked to Rowarth? jammed (— I mean this kind of :—) swammed, or done any thing else ordinary or ex- traordinary? Many black- berries in Hill Hill Hollow this year? No: you usually go to Middlewood for them, don't you.

I have seen a great many sweet chestnuts this year. The

3/ Drive at Fleet is covered with them, & pheasants, too. Also there is a very fine show of holly berries — you might think Christmas Day was next week for they are scarlet already.

Not many green buses on Saturdays owing to the working-to-rule business, & on a couple of Friday mornings if you had been travelling towards Plymouth about 10.30 am you might have seen an angular figure signalling to passing cars for a ride. (Fridays too have sometimes been without a bus from Paington to Plymouth.) Of course there is always the 🚲

Did I tell you what a school girl I know said when she saw me come out with my cycle for the first time? Esme is